The Worst

SHITFACED

Phenomenal Swear Word To Color

For Stress Releasing

C.J. Willoughby

I0463961

Happy Coloring!

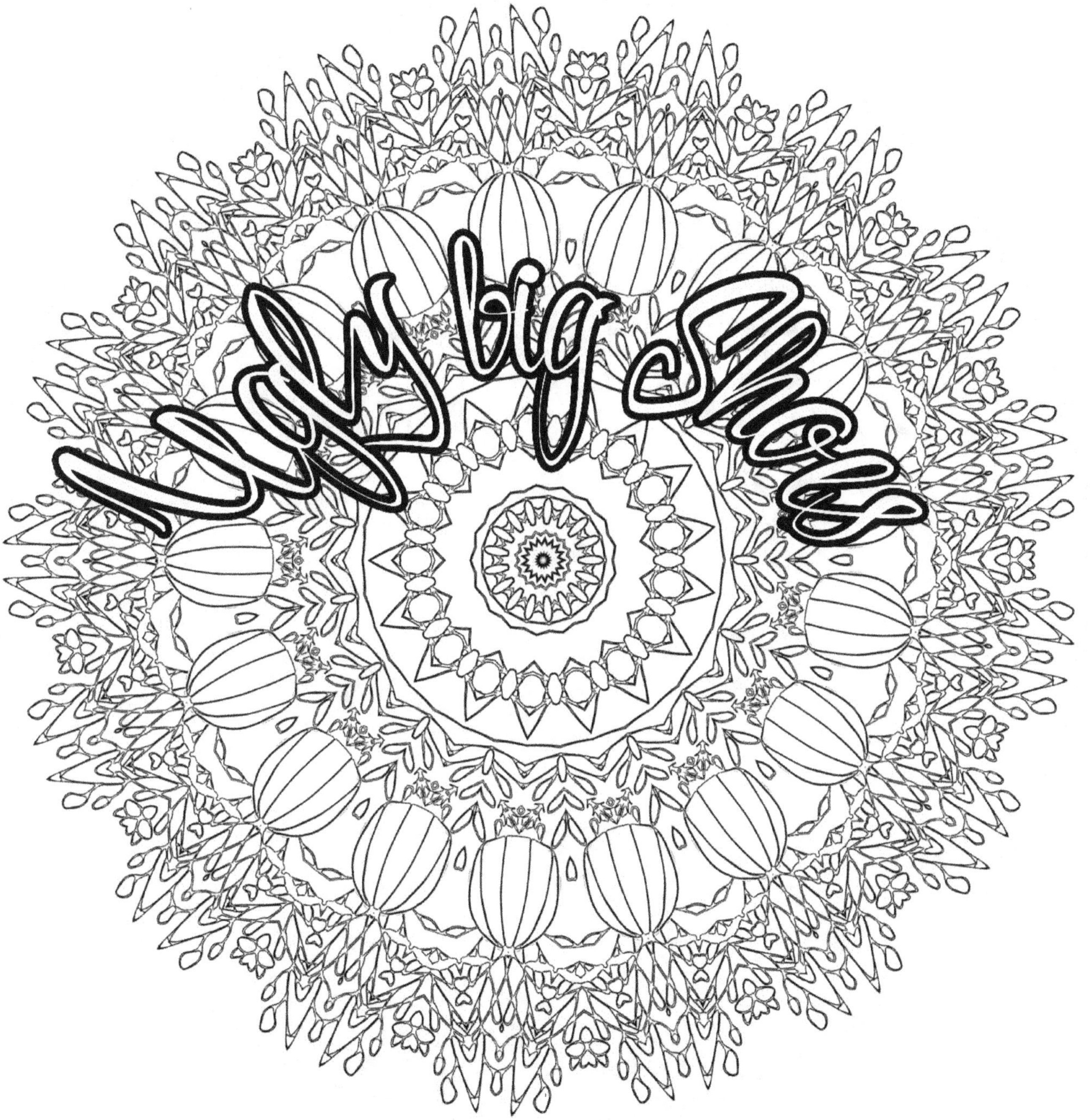
Ugly big Shoes

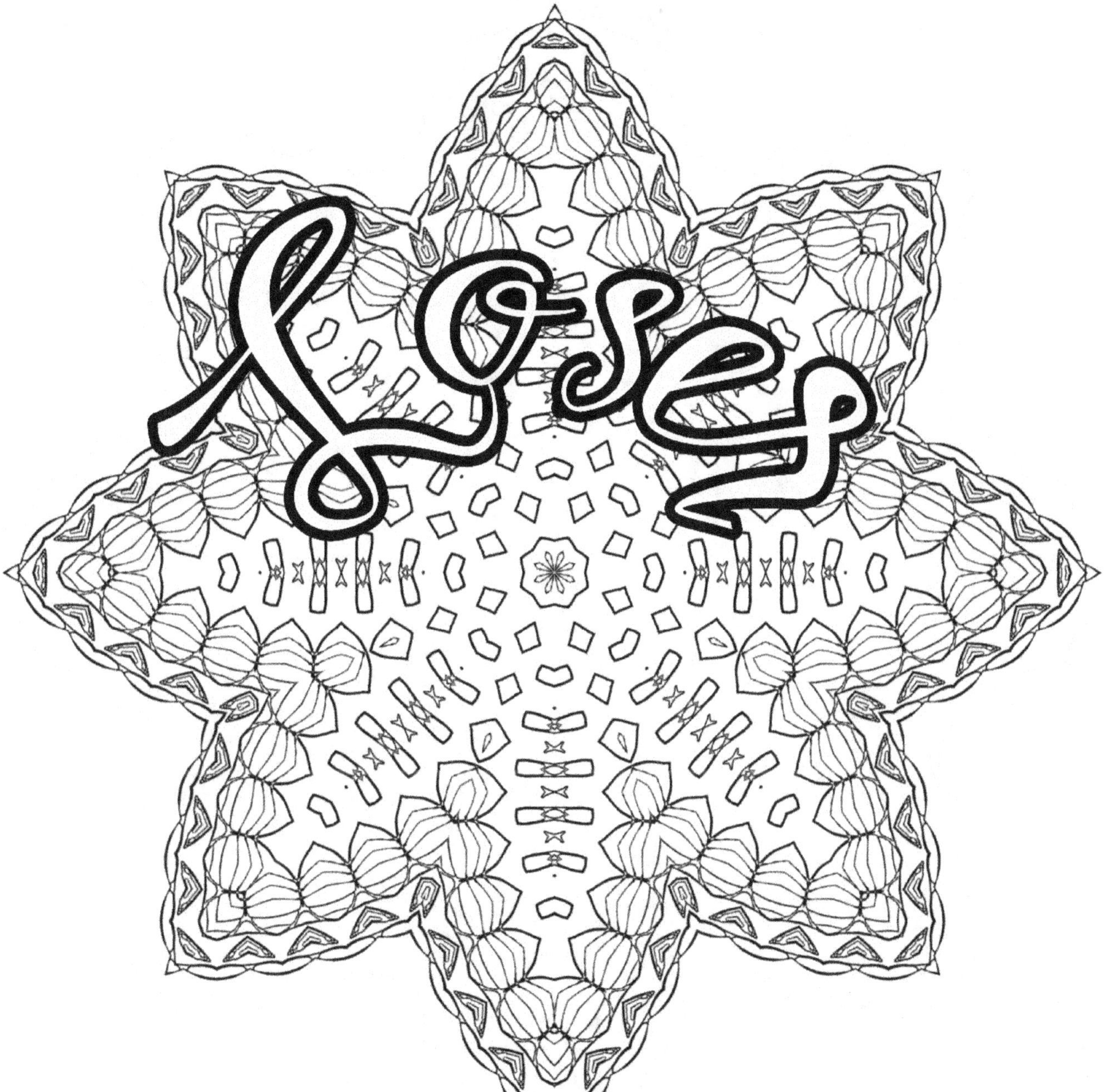
Loser

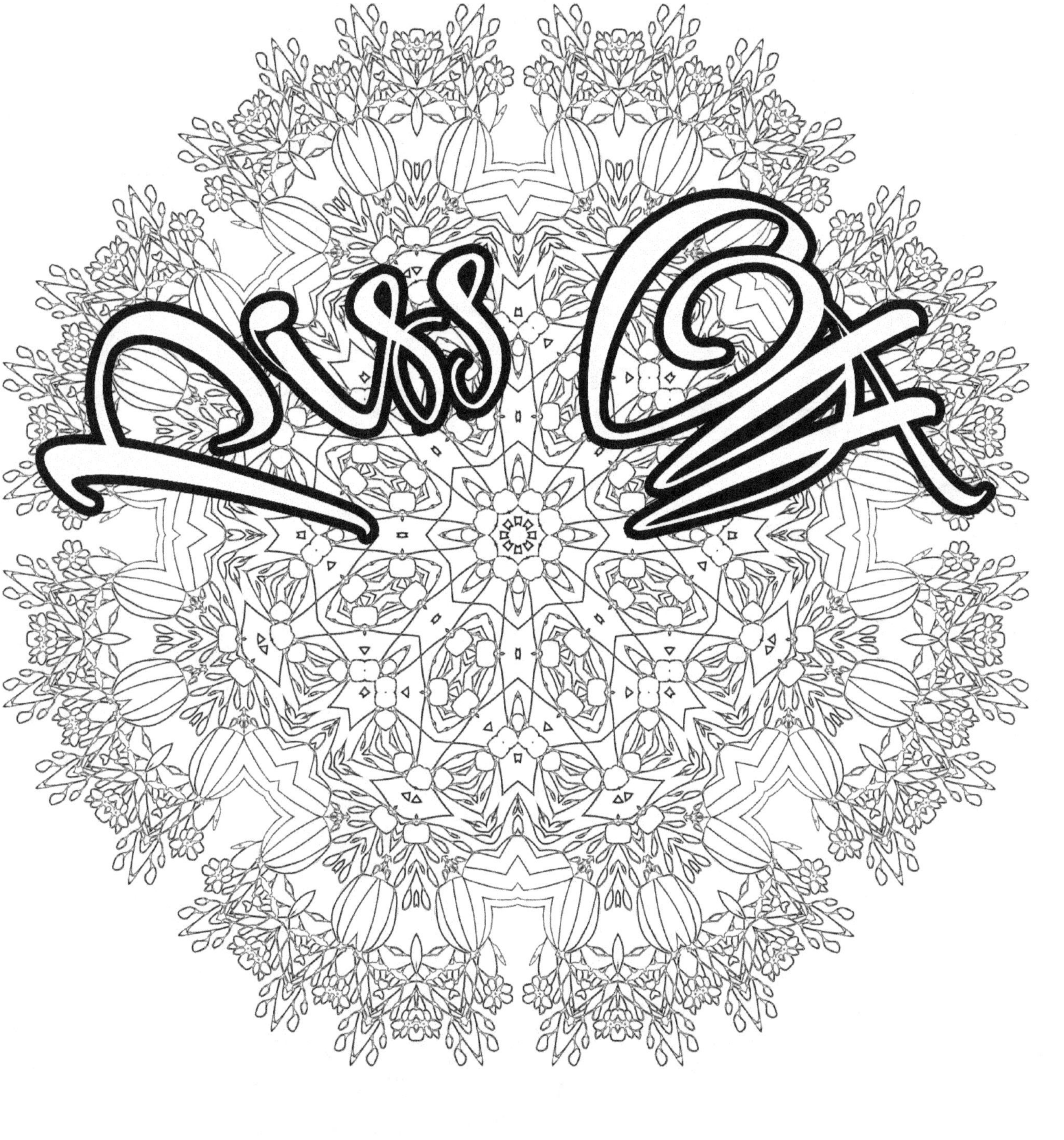
Piss Off

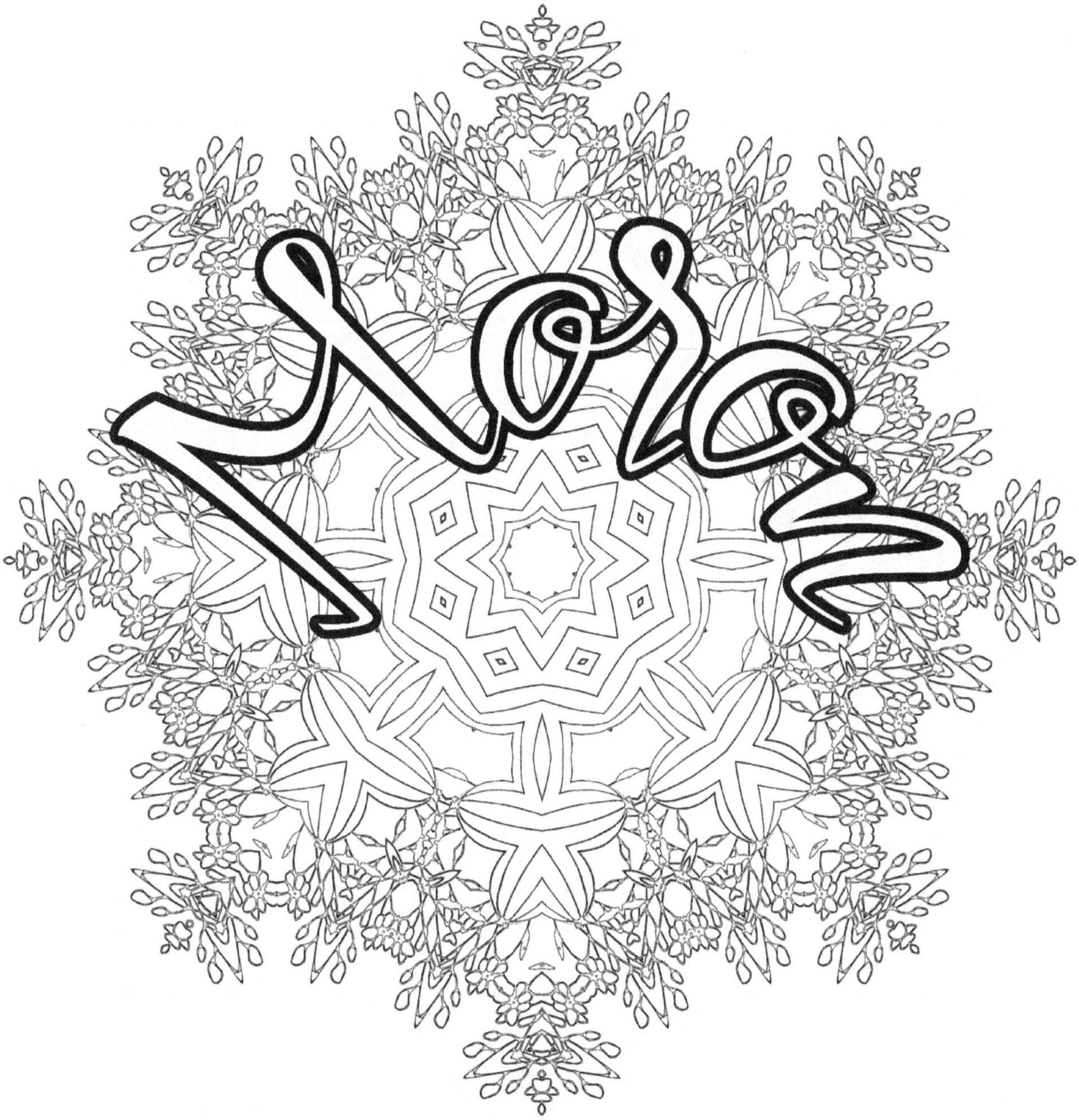

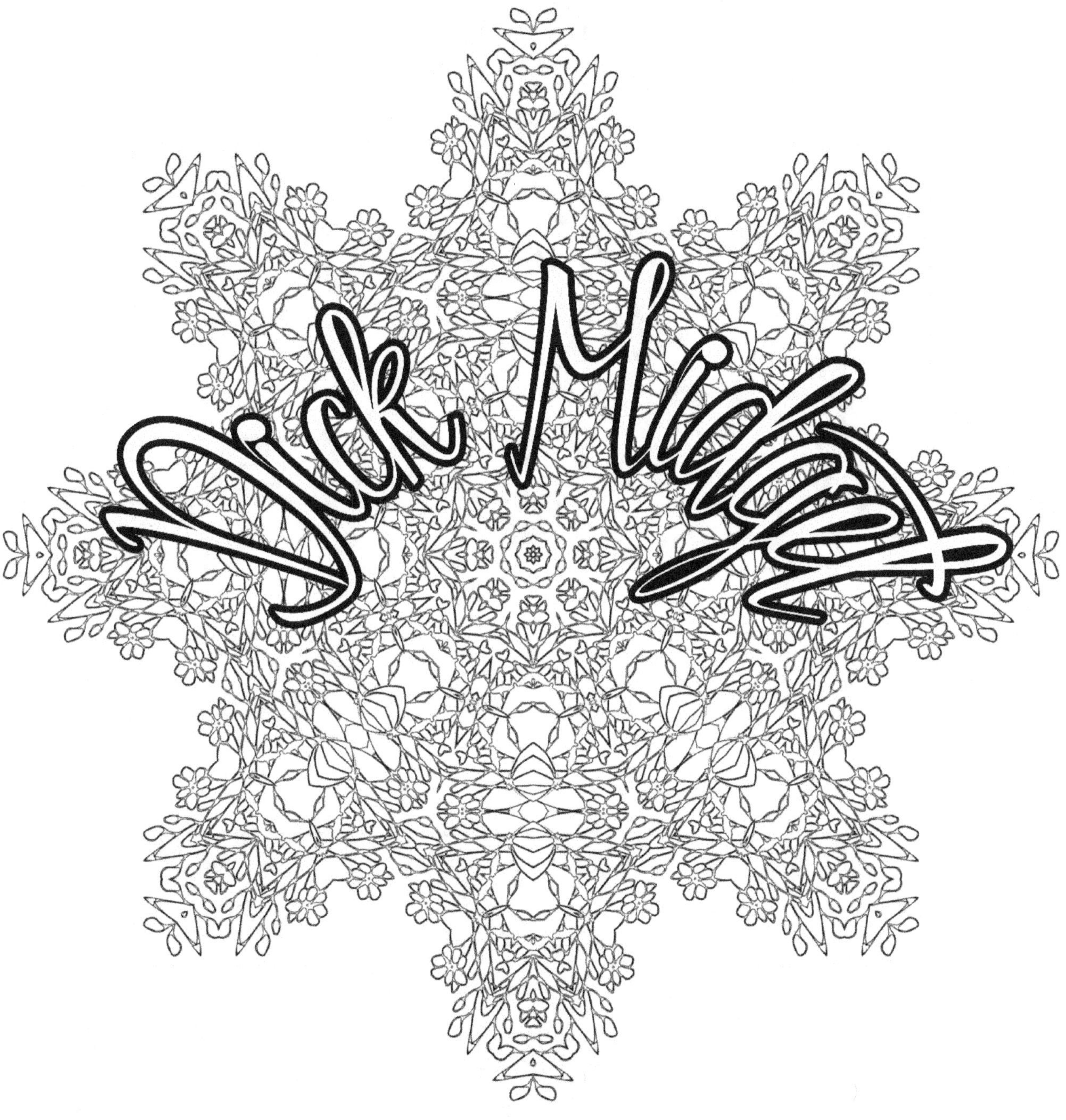
Dick Midget

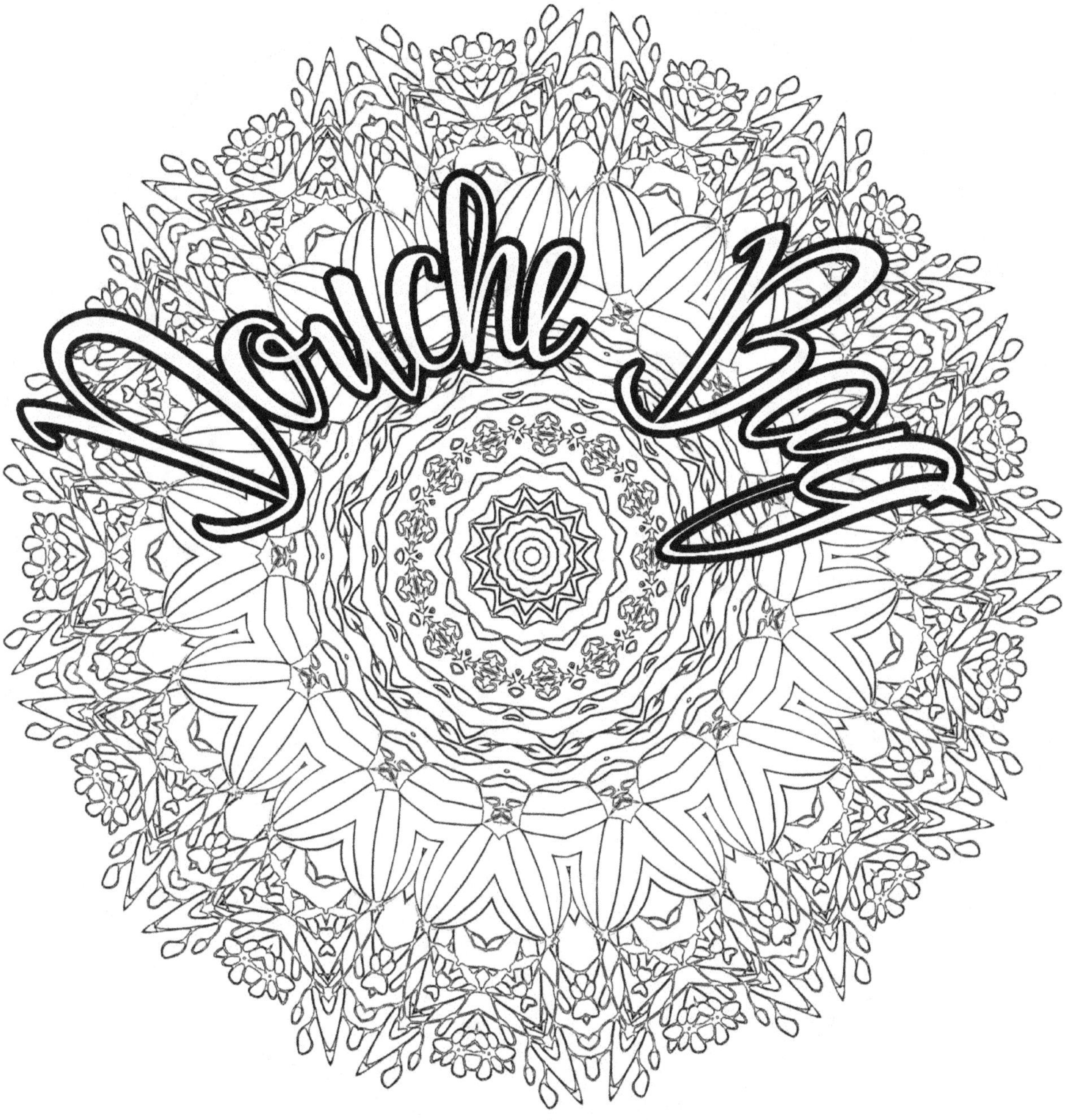
Douche Bag

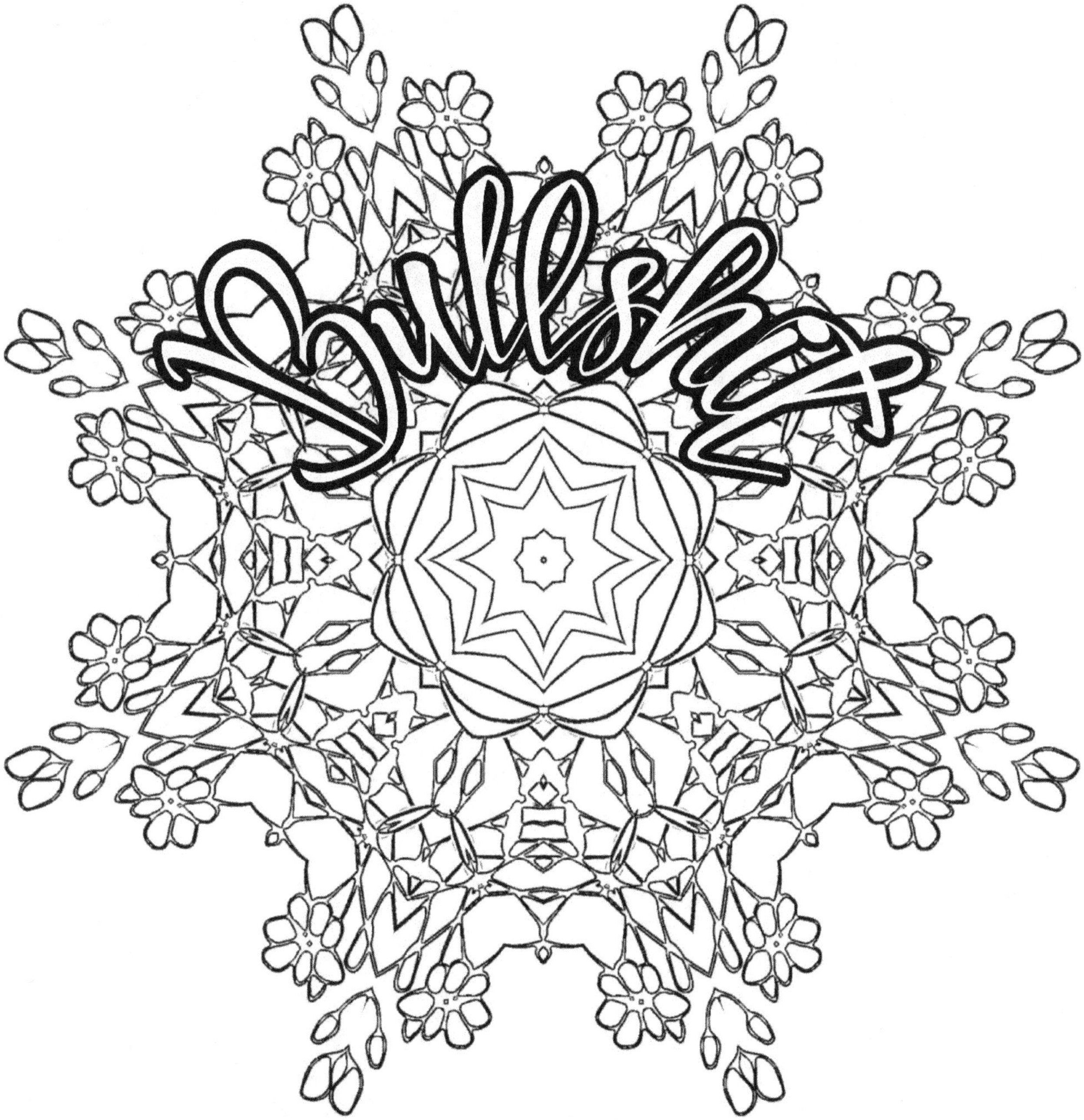
Bullshit

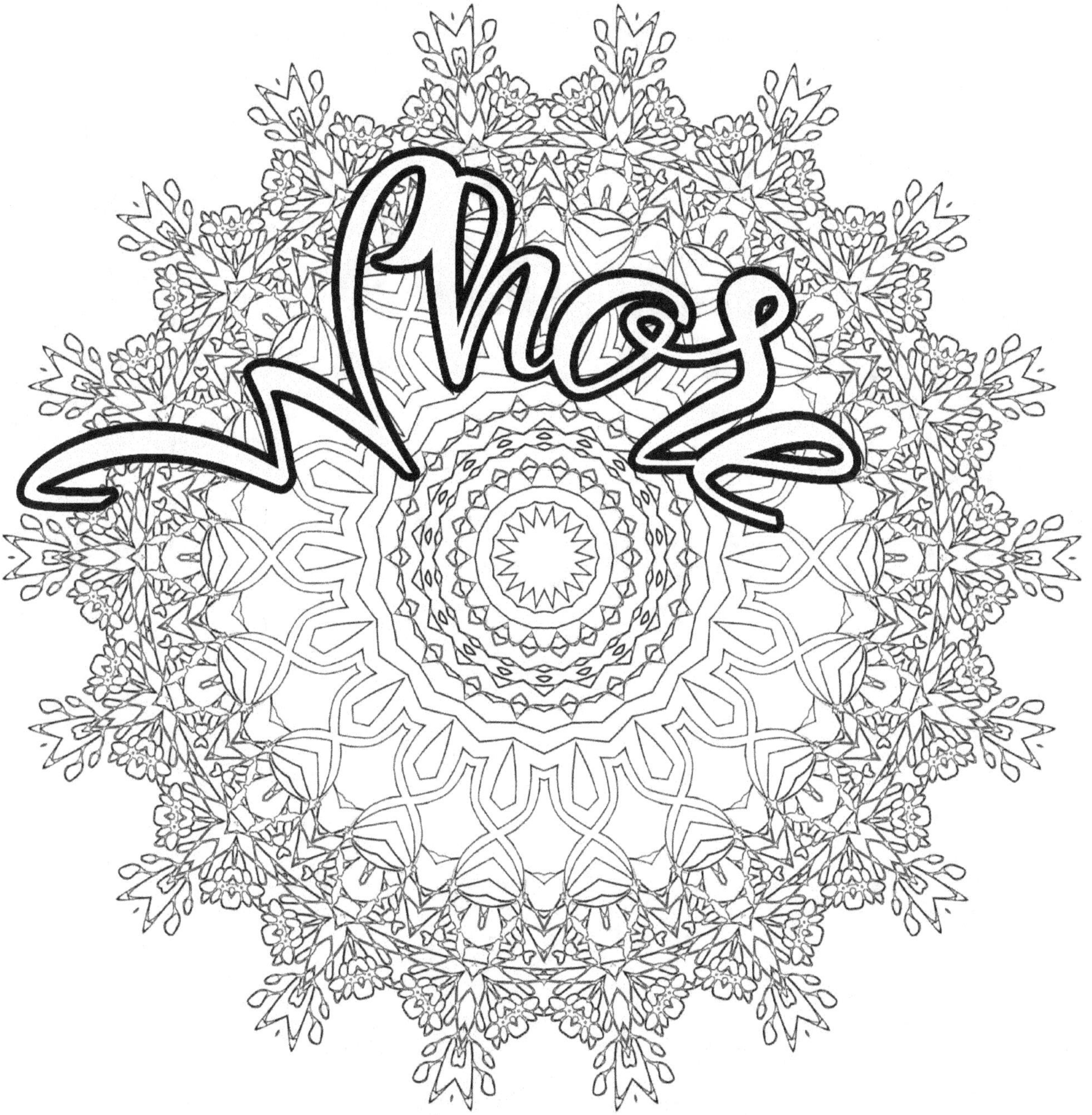
Whore

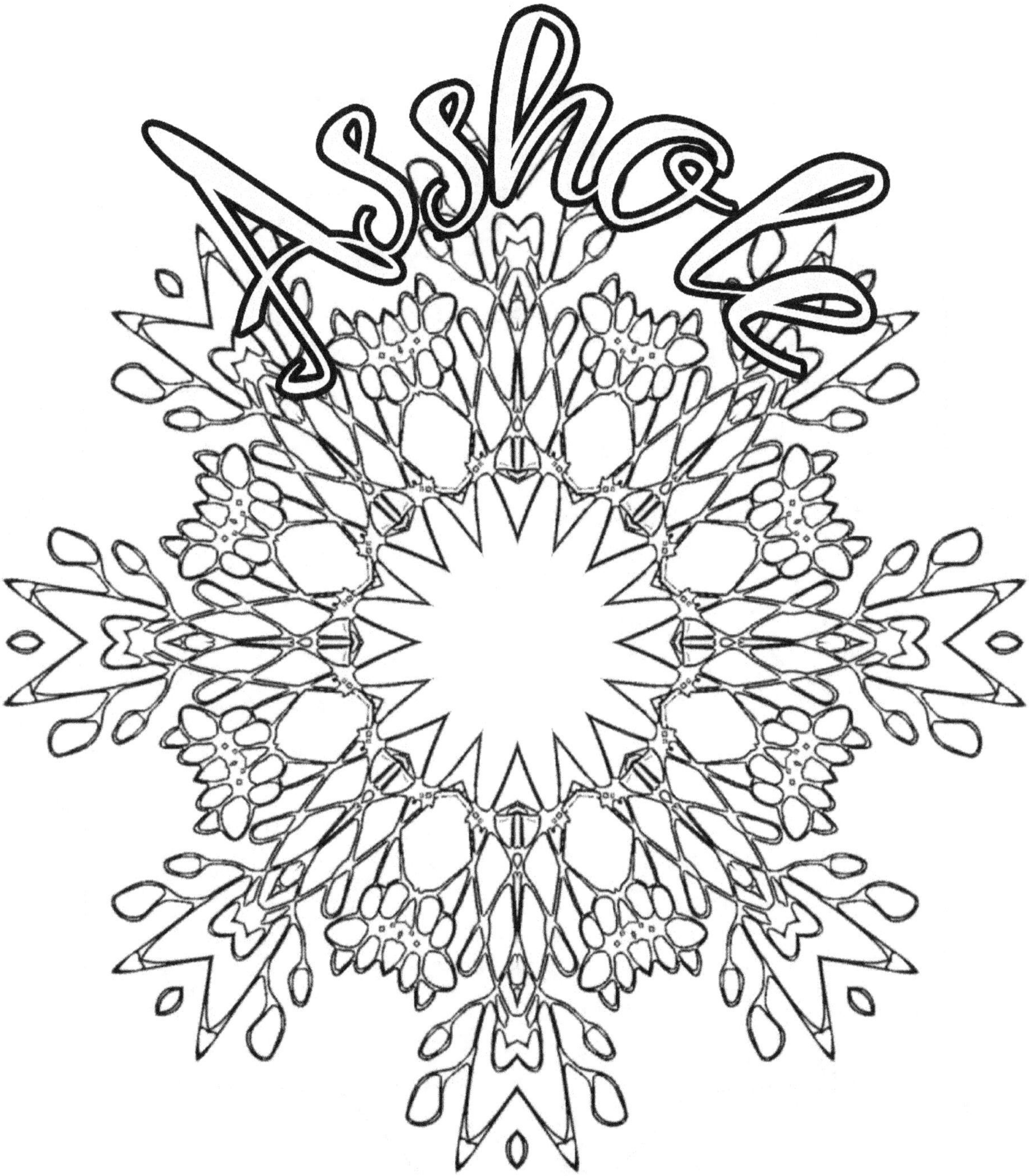
Asshole

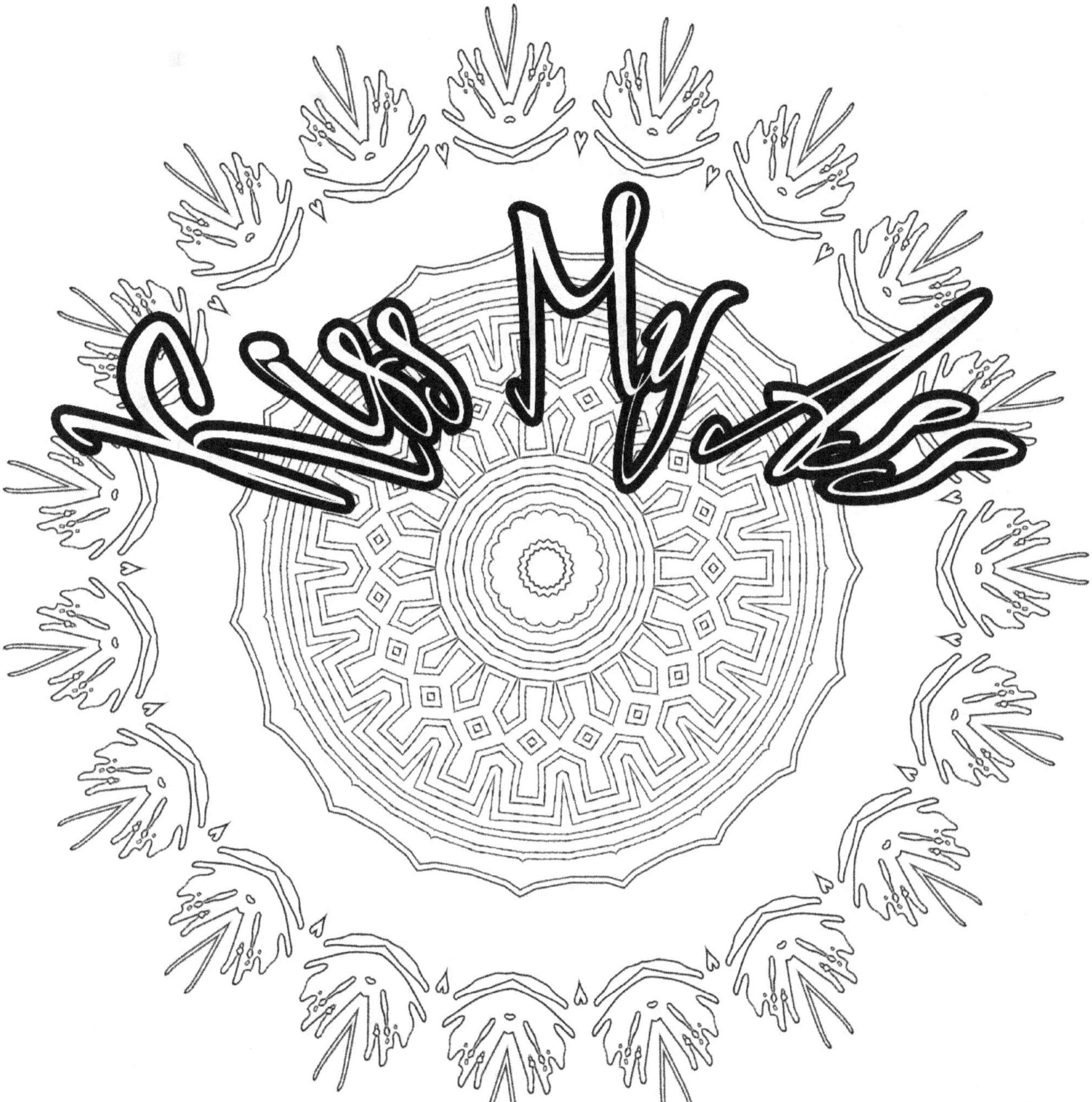
Kiss My Ass

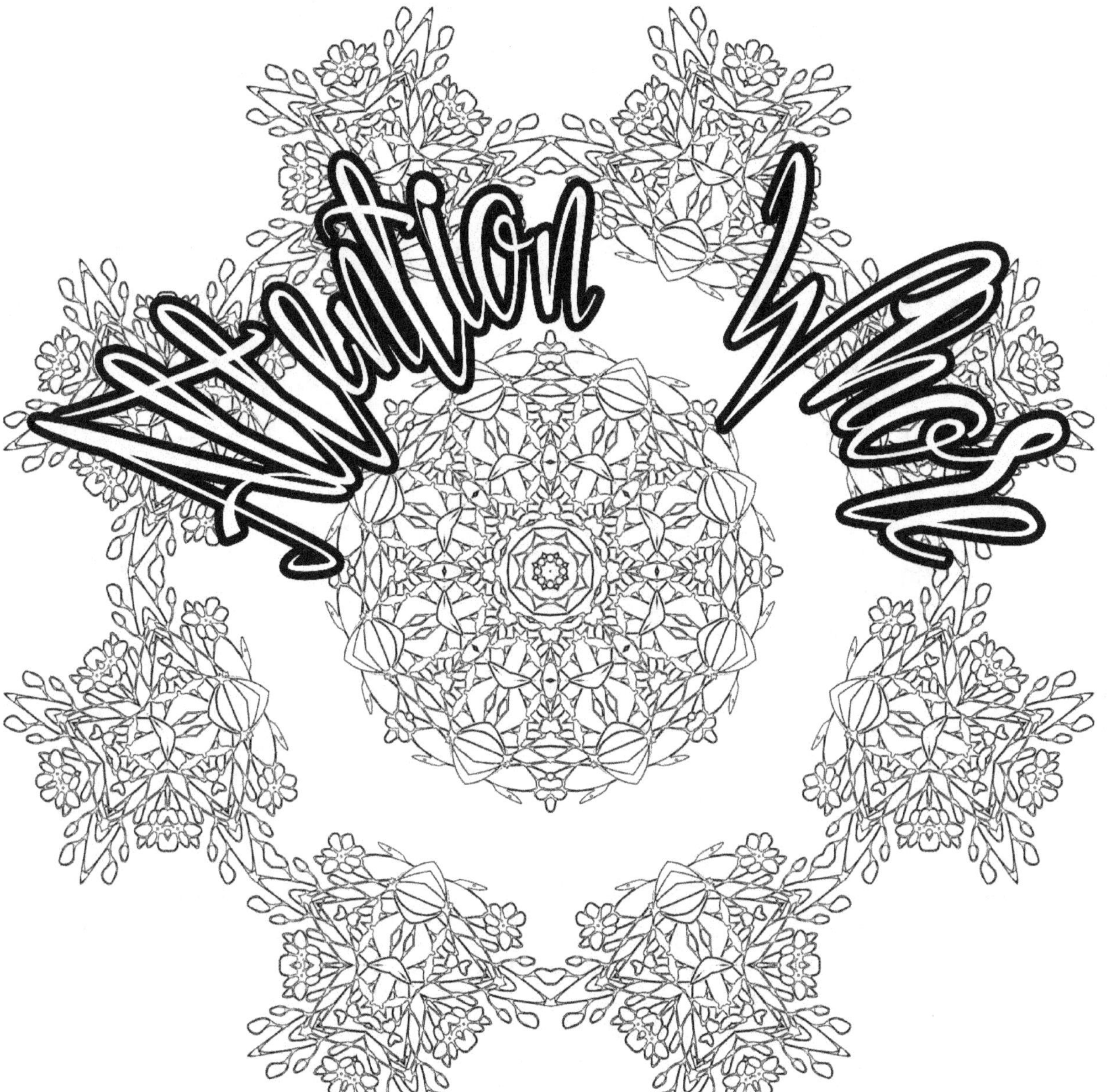
Nutrition Week

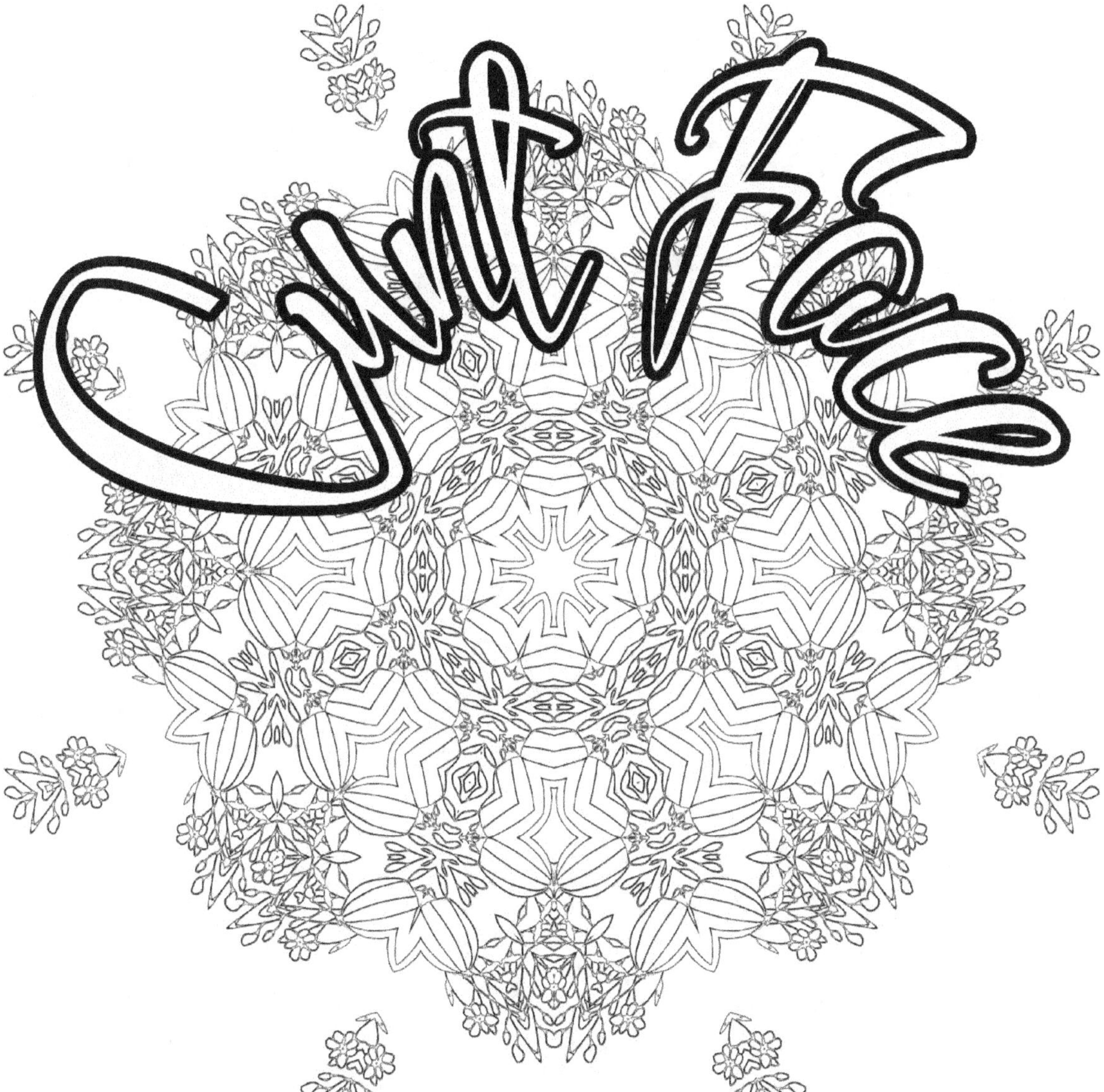
Cunt Face

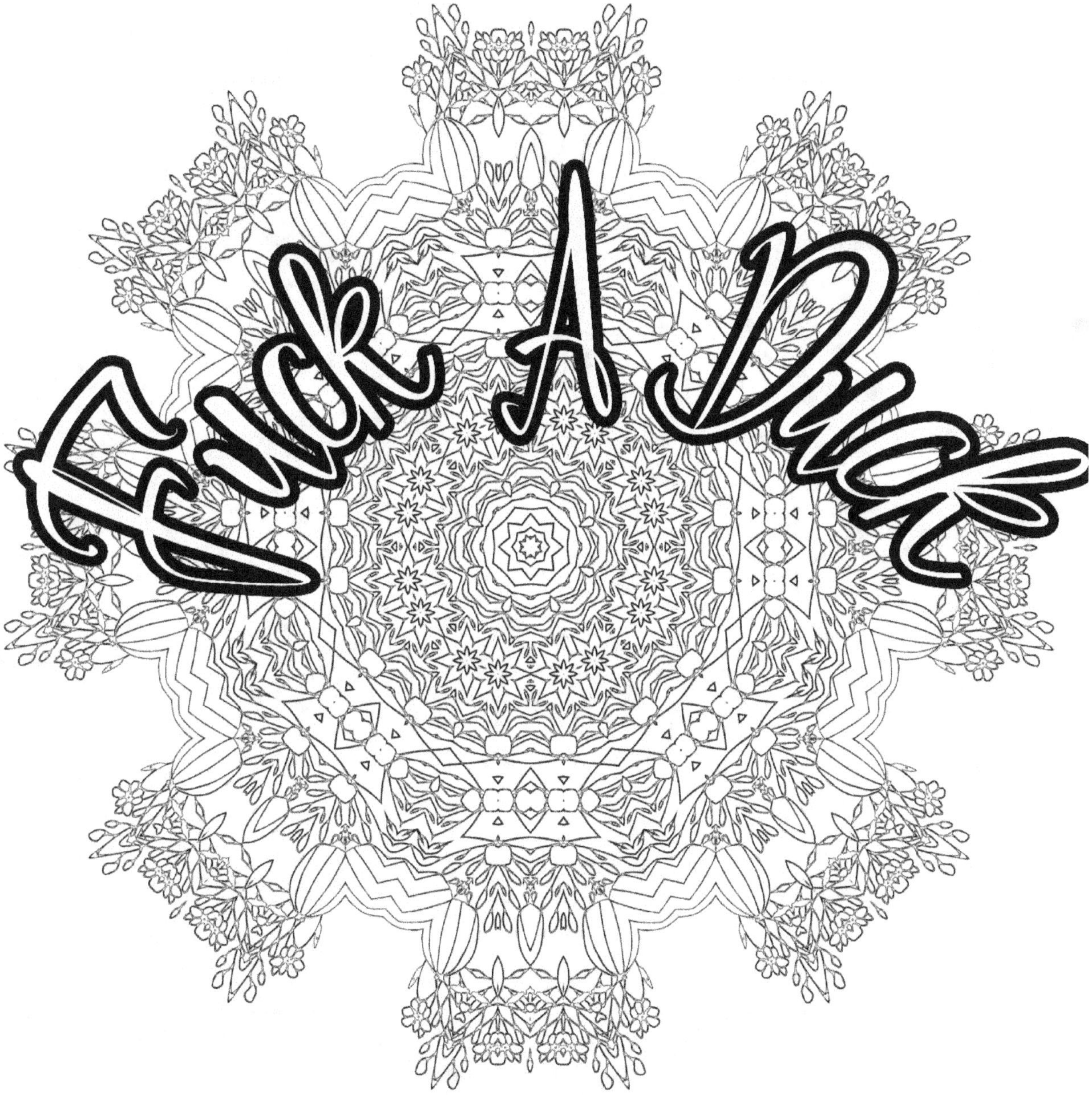
Fuck A Duck

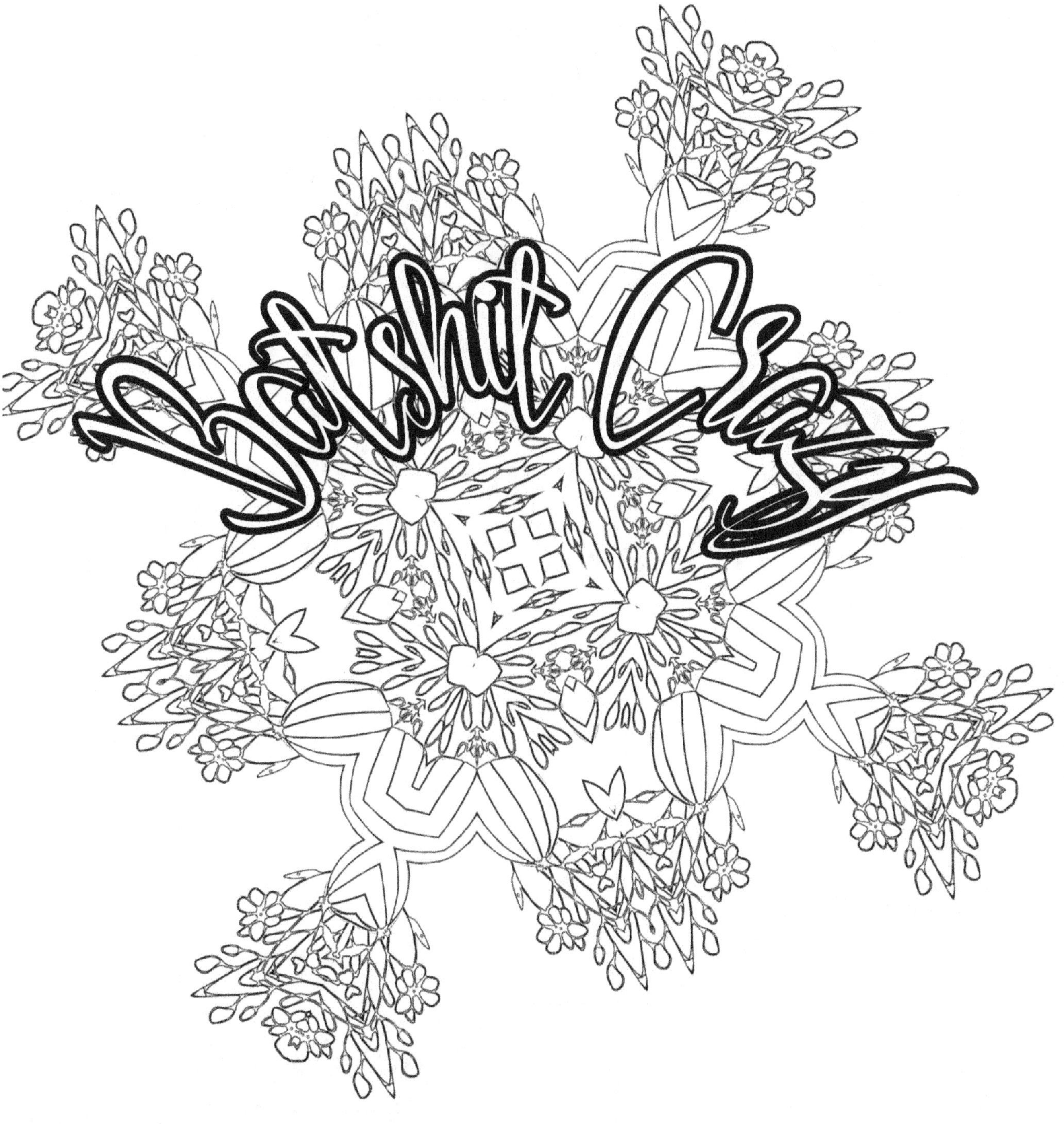
Batshit Crazy

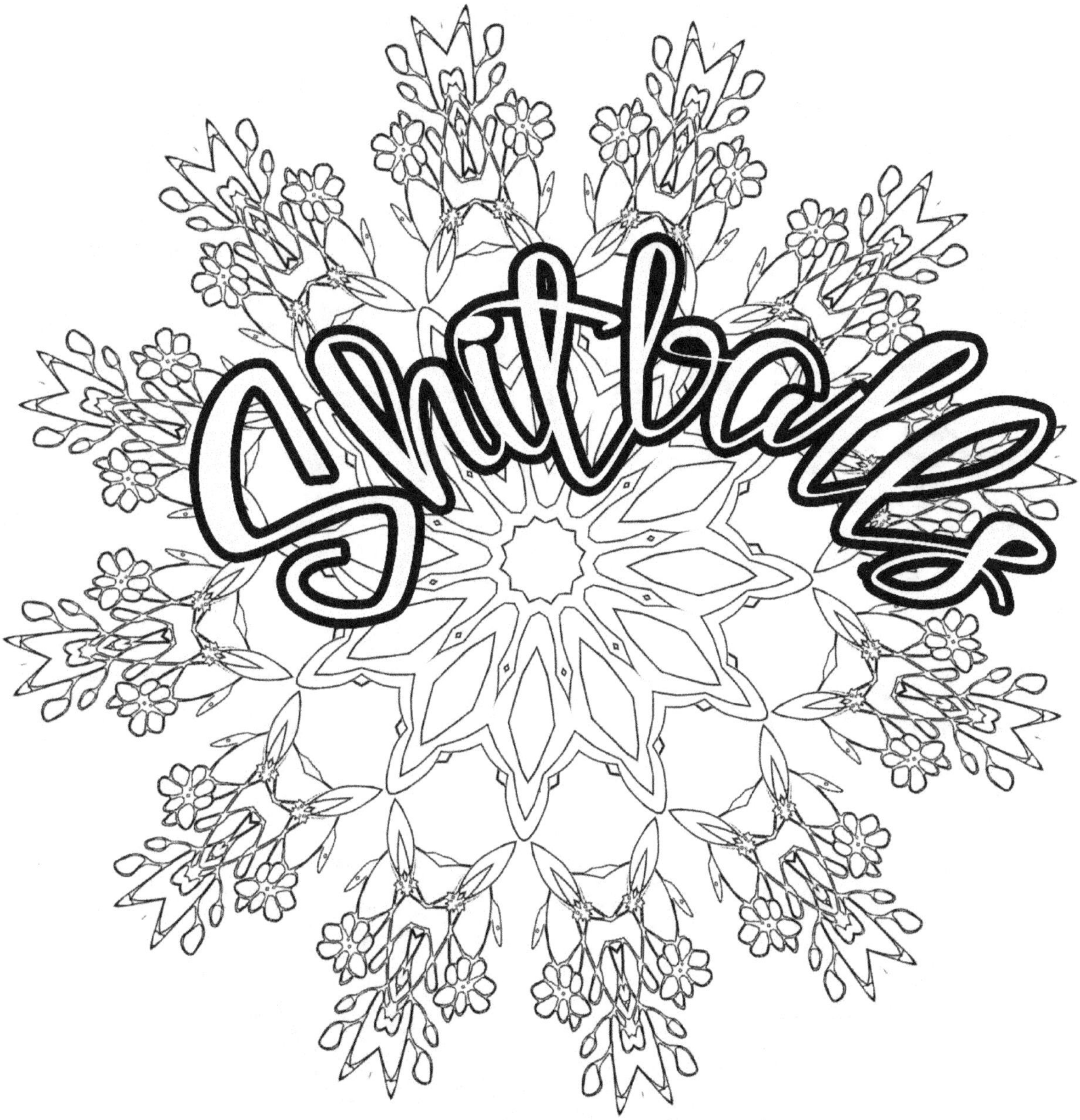
Shitballs

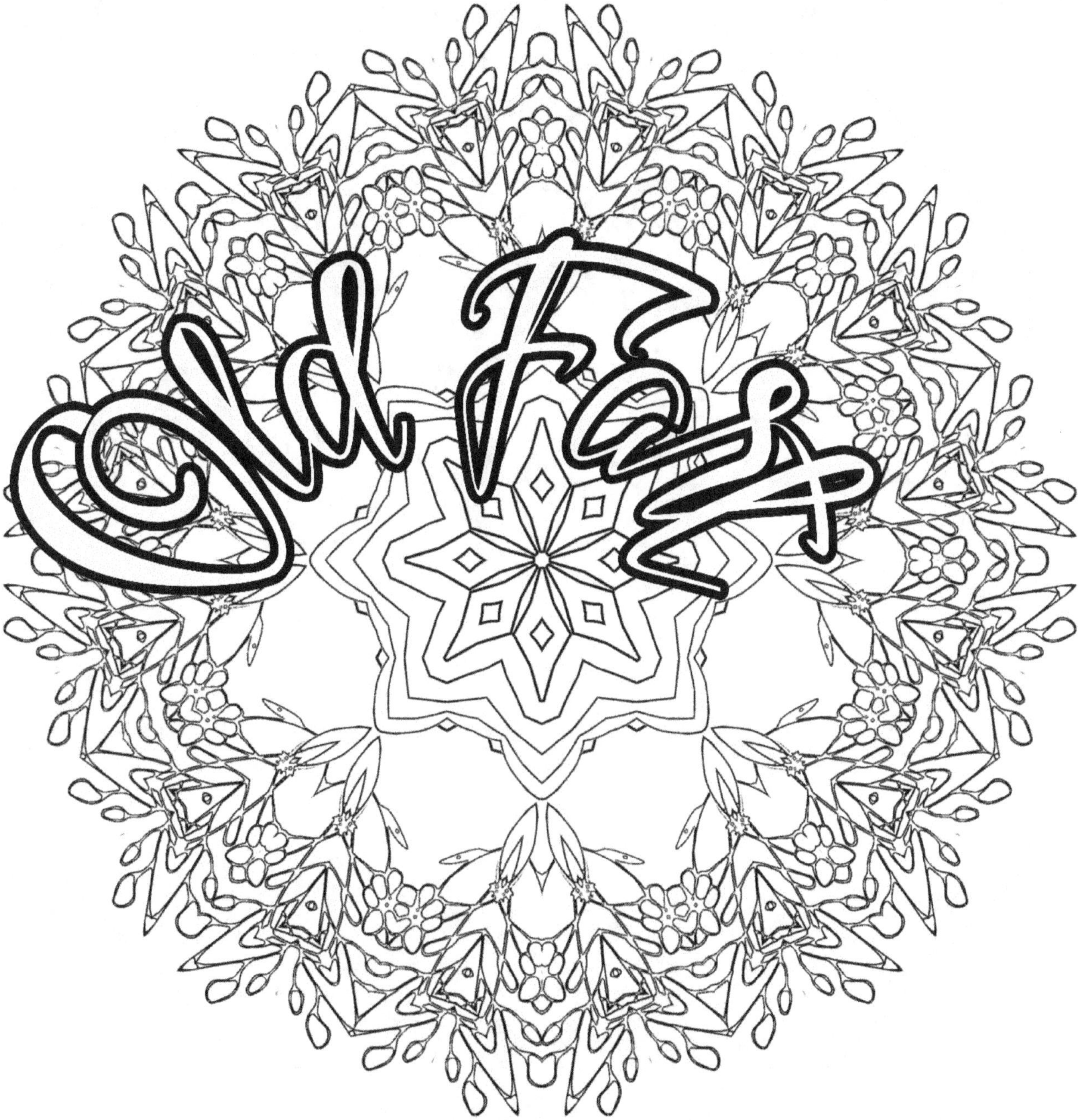
Old Fart

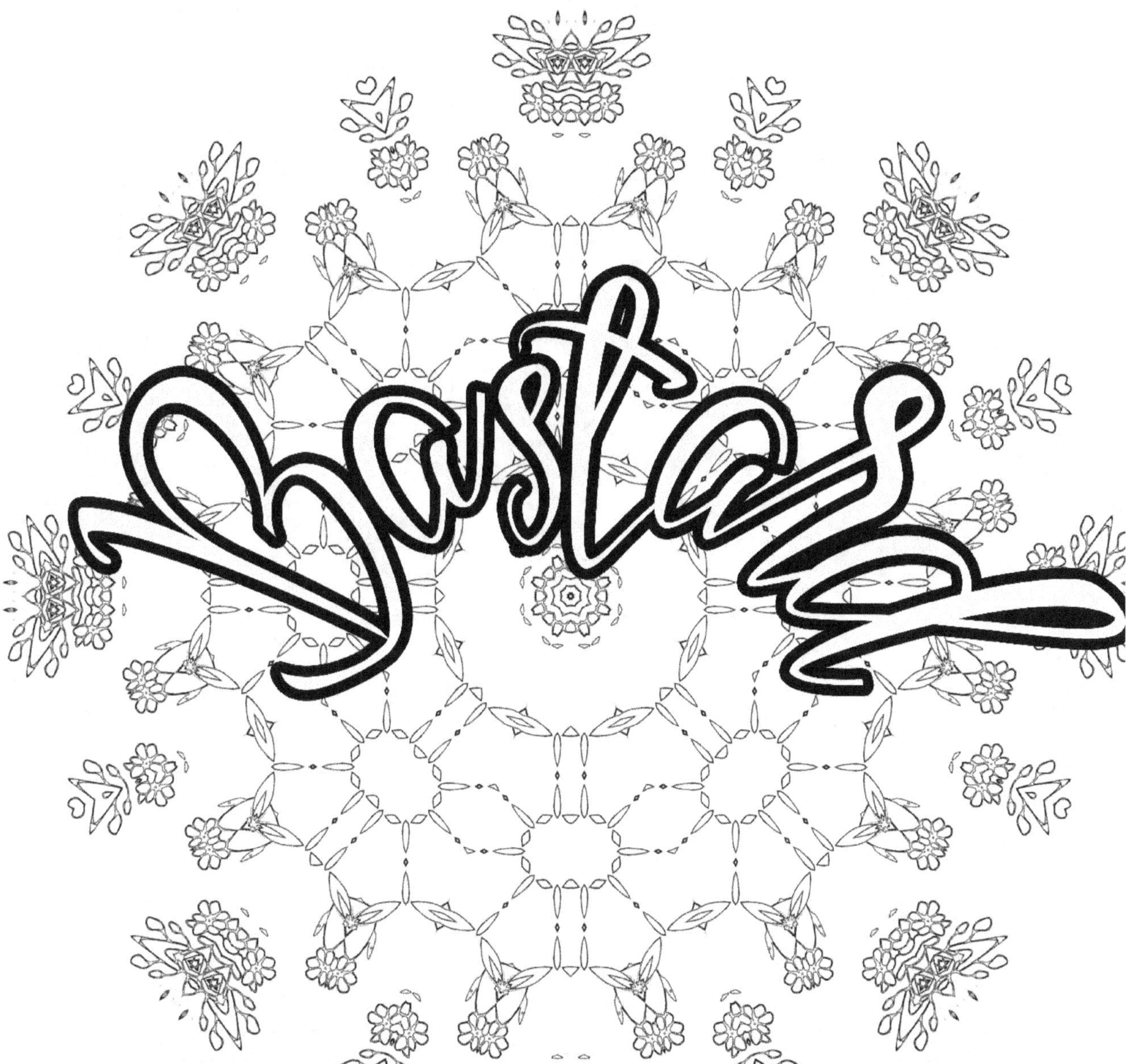
bastard

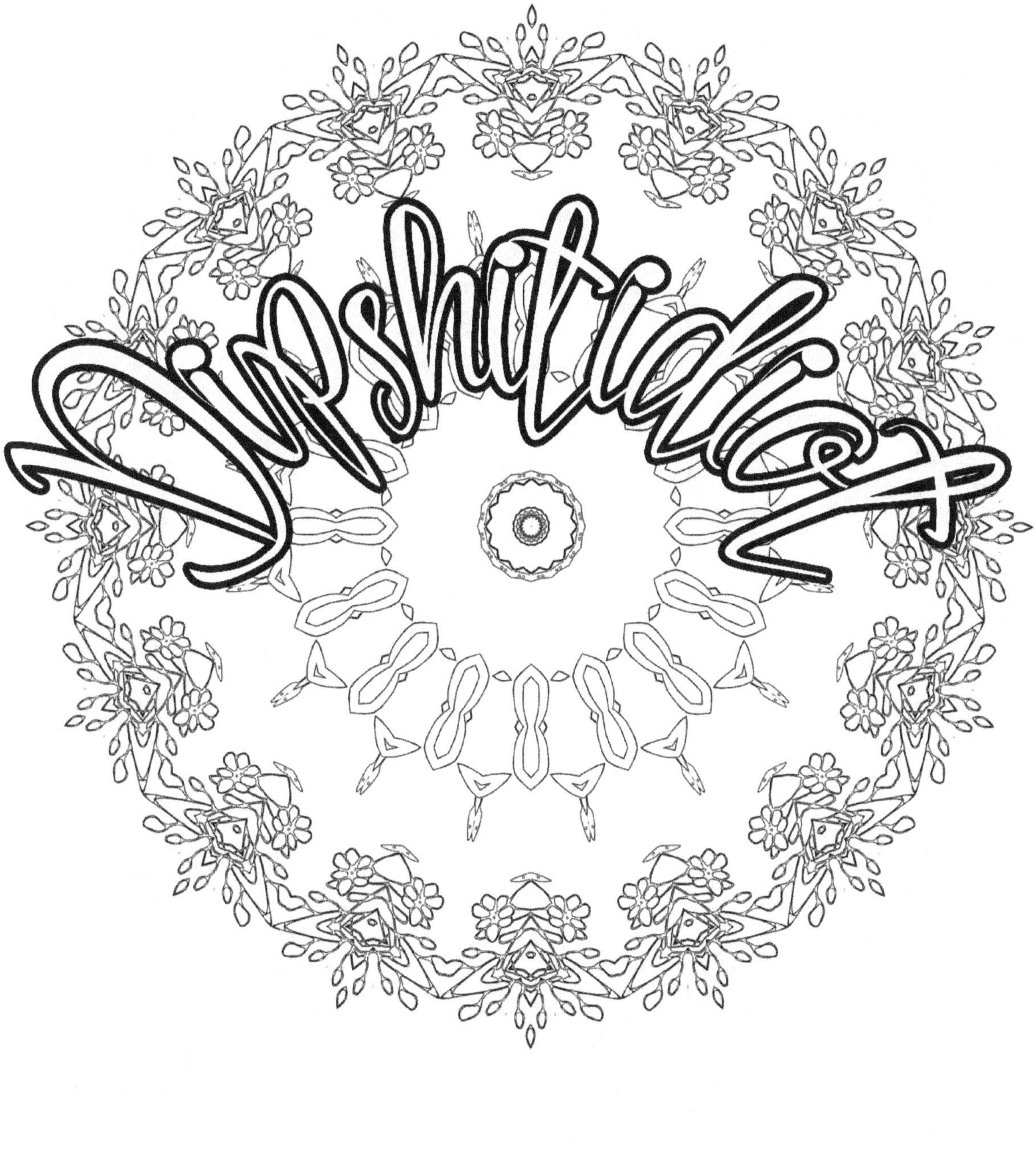
Dipshitidiot

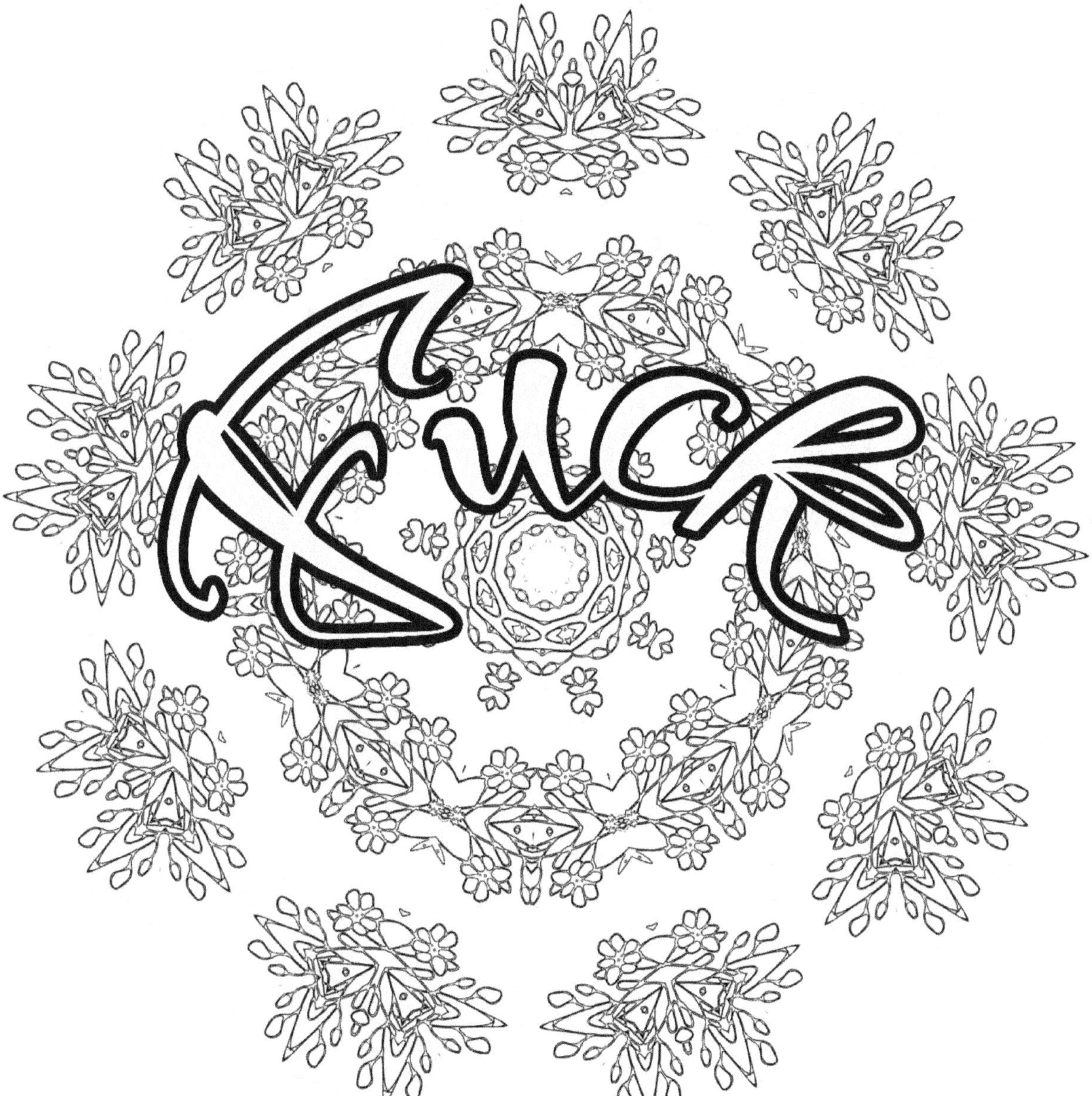
Fuck

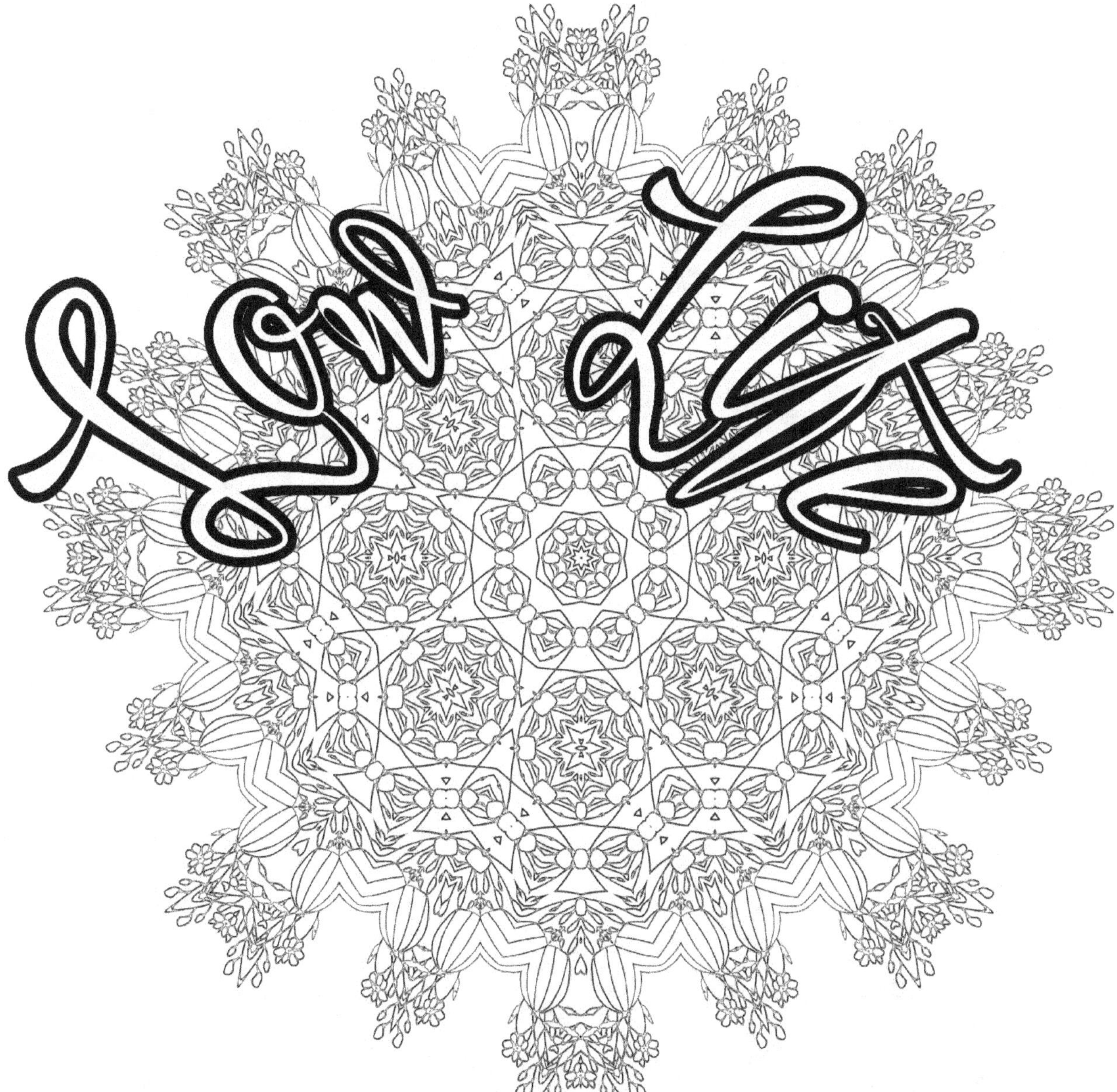
Love Life

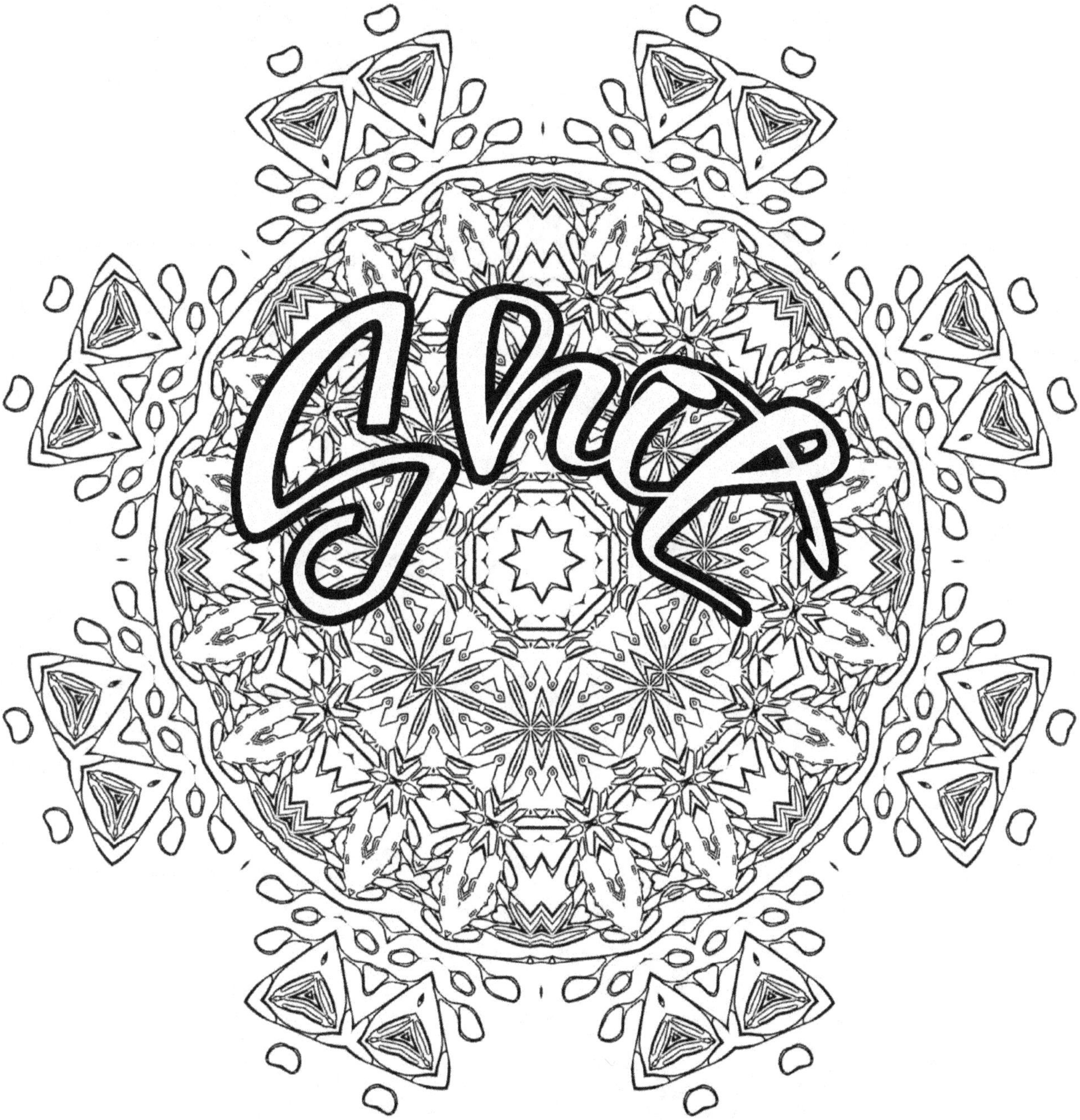
Shit

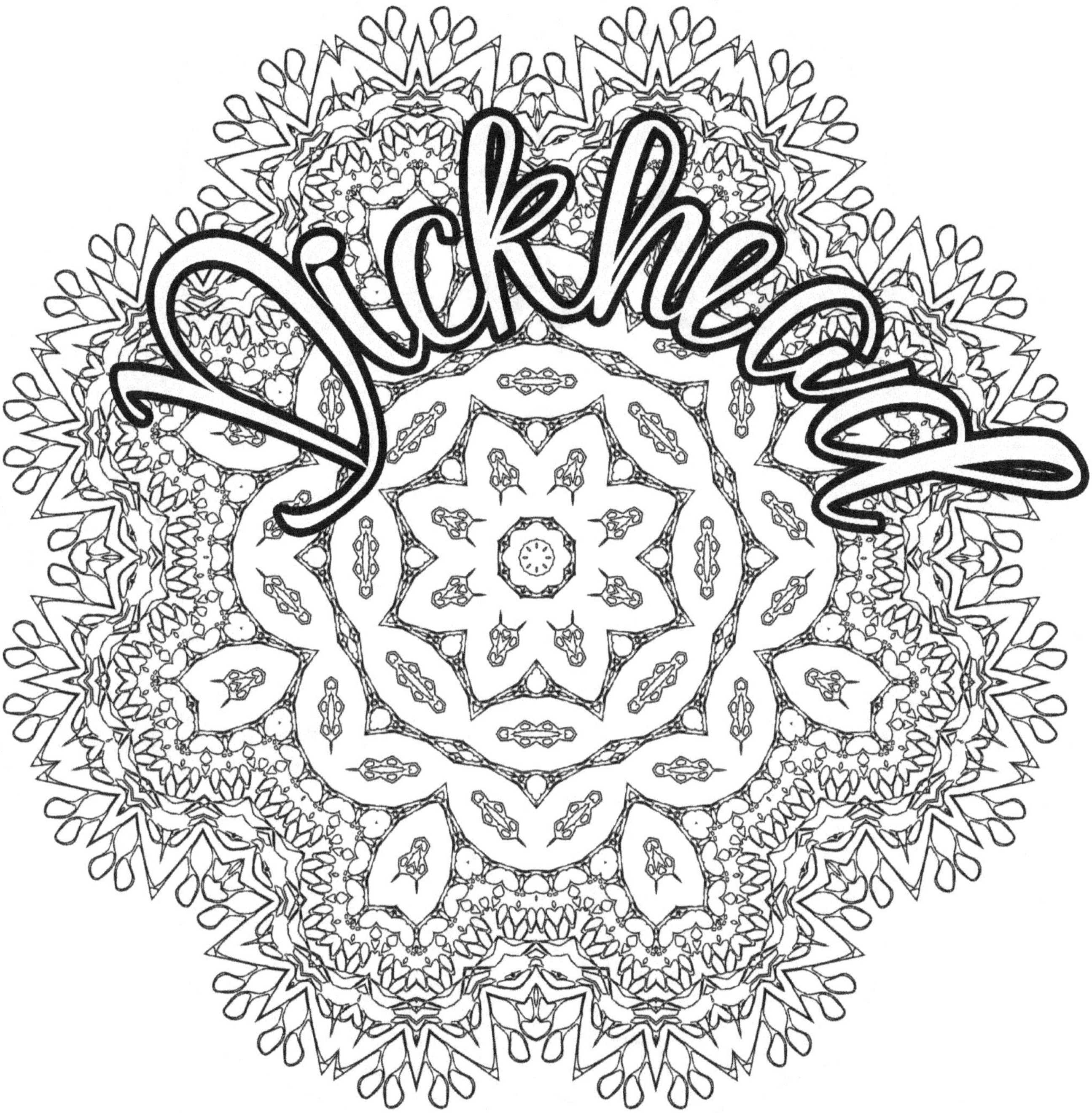
Dickhead

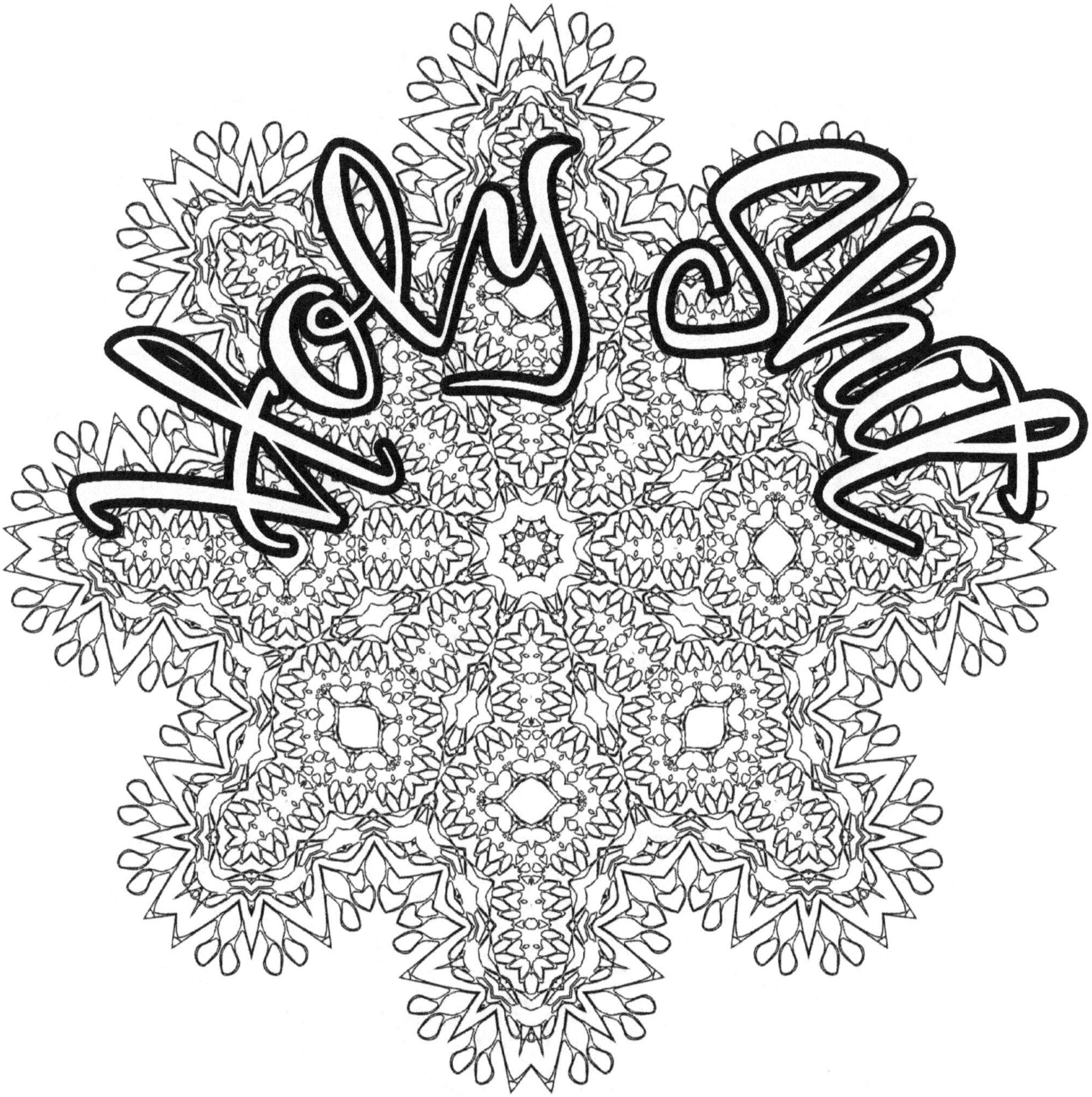
Holy Shit

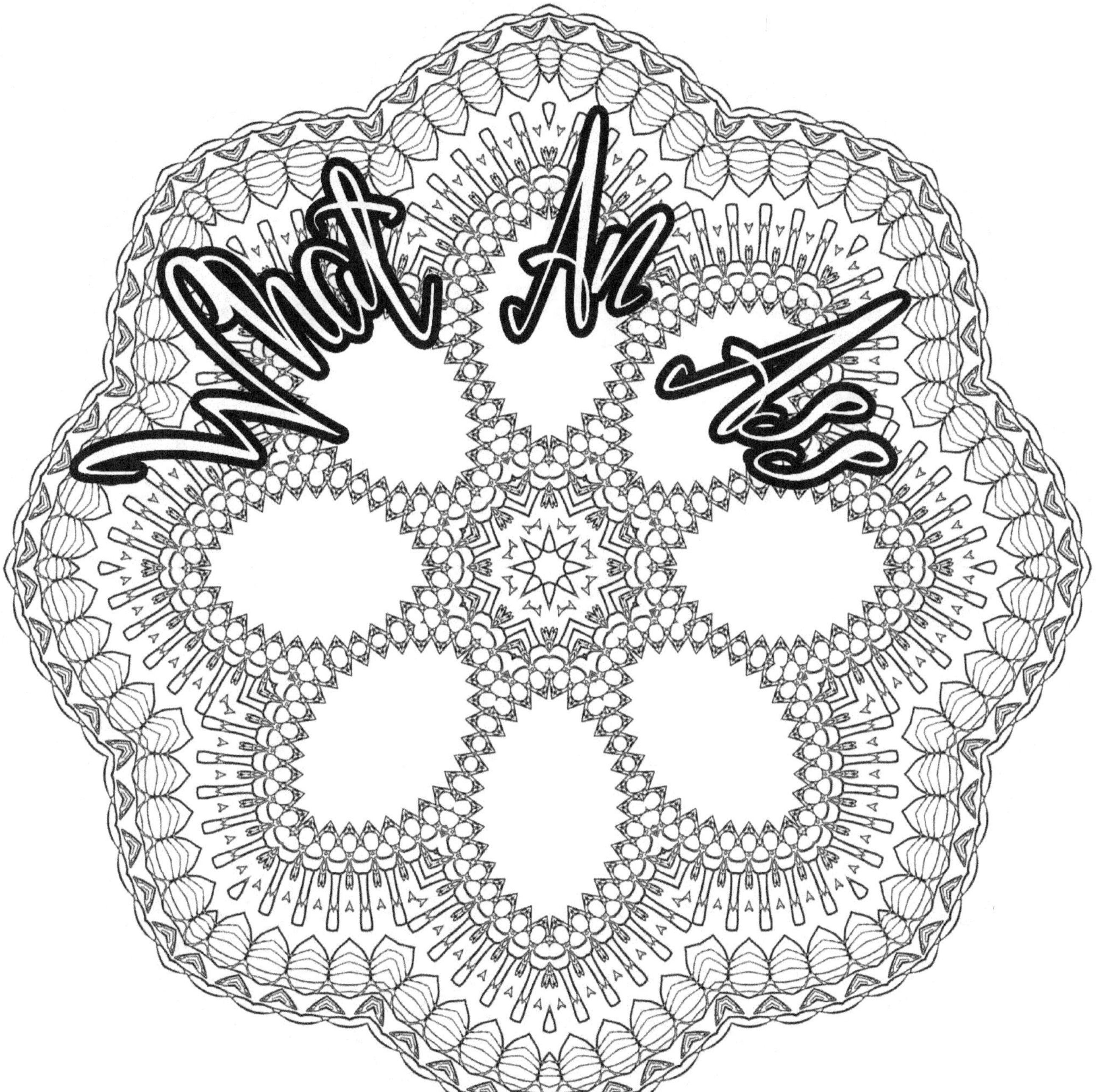
What An Ass

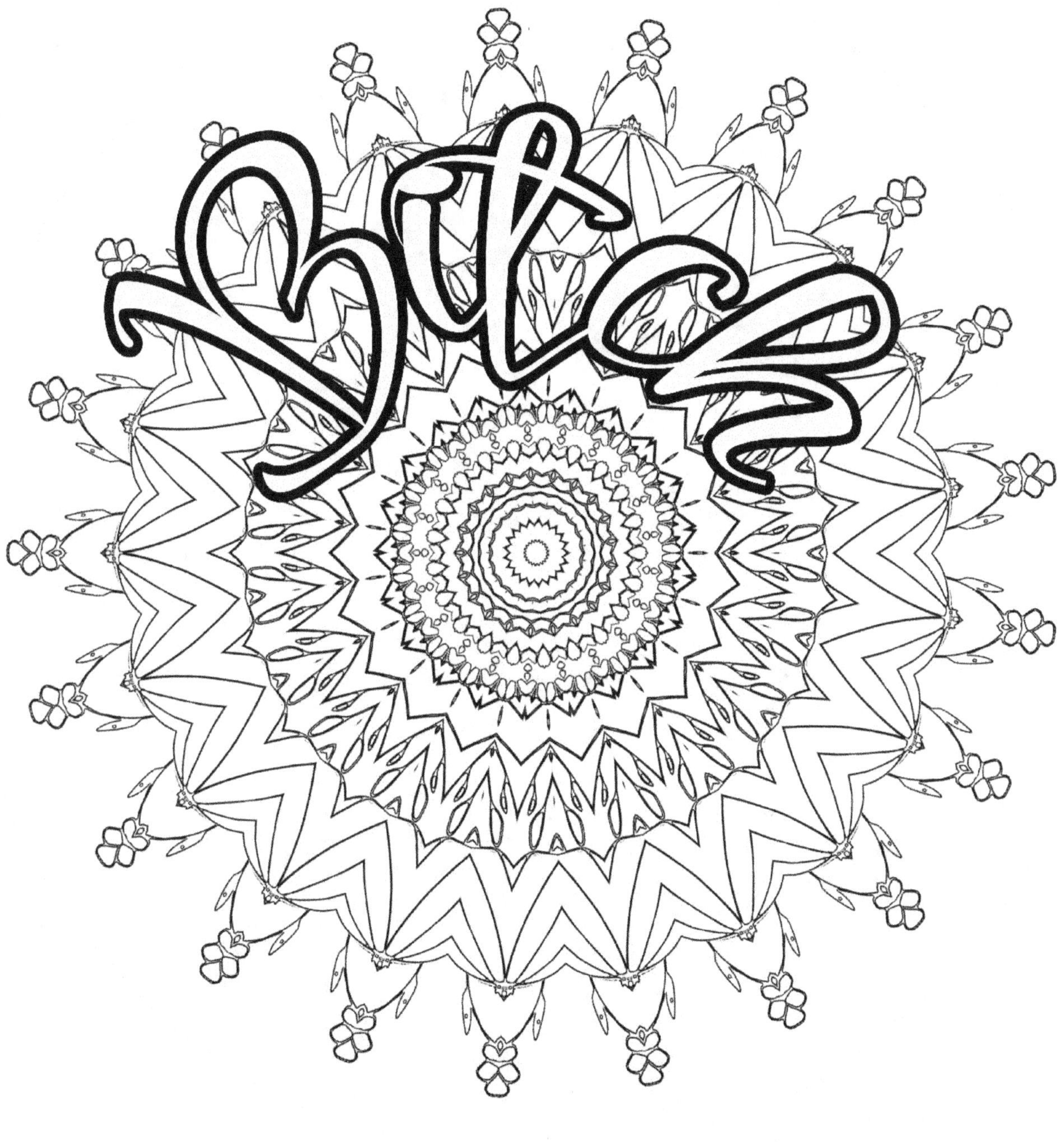
Bitch

www.ingramcontent.com/pod-product-compliance
Lightning Source LLC
Chambersburg PA
CBHW081750170526
45167CB00009B/3987
9781544062051